G000122816

MAIDCHILLA
MANUAL

BRIDECHILLA

Help grow the Bridechilla movement,
tag a #**BRIDECHILLA** or a #**MAIDCHILLA**
and spread the word!

Join the Bridechilla Community on Facebook to meet
like-minded Bridechillas and Groomchillas. It's the best
gosh darn wedding planning community around.

Follow Bridechilla on
Facebook @bridechillapodcast
Instagram @bridechillapodcast
Twitter @bridechillapod
Pinterest @bridechillapod

ISBN 9781999916343

Illustrations by Robby Satria. Find him on Instagram @obicatlia
Printed in China

Bridechilla® is registered in the US Patent and Trademark Office.
Copyright © 2018 Happy Days Media Inc., Aleisha McCormack

Happy Days Media Inc. 2018
www.thebridechilla.com

Welcome, Maidchilla
Surviving the rollercoaster of wedding planning.

WELL, LOOK AT YOU! You are the chosen one. Your friend holds you in such high esteem that she has selected *you* for the duty of being a bridesmaid. Or perhaps a maid of honor, or co-maid of honor if she really didn't want to draw battle lines, or co-co-maid of honor if she has no lady balls and just 'sees you all as equal'. In Bridechilla-land, we call bridesmaids 'Maidchillas'. You are a trusted gal-pal, a maker of memories, and an in-joke vault.

Whatever the moniker, you have been selected to be a Bridechilla sidekick, to get frocked up together, most likely in a dress of their choosing. If your Bridechilla friend is particularly modern, perhaps your opinion will be noted. You may be asked to select from a number of dresses as if you were on *The Price Is Right*. Choose wisely my friend, choose wisely. Regardless, you will most likely be required to pay for said dress, and after its day in the spotlight, it will find a special place in the back of the closet next to all the other outfits that you keep for nostalgic purposes and will try on once every three years and yet still keep because it feels wrong to throw them out.

But being a Maidchilla isn't all about the dress. A modern Maidchilla wears many hats. Party planner, counselor, keeper of secrets...let's be honest, you're basically a one-woman version of the *Queer Eye* team and for that I salute you. You may be an experienced Maidchilla or a newbie to this wedding planning scene, but either way, every wedding (and Bridechilla) is different, as are the expectations of the event and your involvement in it.

Having been a bridesmaid on a number of occasions and having heard thousands of real life bridal party wins and sagas through the Bridechilla Community on Facebook, I want this handbook to be a beacon of support for you. This guide will help you help your friend through the wedding planning process, and make sure that both of you come out the other side stronger, able to laugh off any drama and hopefully have a couple of great dinner party stories to tell.

HOW TO MAINTAIN YOUR MAIDCHILLA CHILL... EVEN WHEN SHIT GETS TENSE

Here's the thing, there's no *one way* to be a Maidchilla. Soz. There is no rulebook, no list of must dos. If you visit a bunch of mainstream wedding forums looking for answers, you may quickly find yourself packing a bag and bailing on this whole commitment altogether, because being a bridesmaid for some of those needy forum broads sounds like a complete shitshow.*

We all have different ideas about what being part of a bridal party means and what is expected of us in that role. Often this is where things can go awry.

I recently asked the Bridechilla Community about their expectations for the role of their bridal party – what they'd like them to help out with. The responses were a mixed bag. Some Chillas had a very firm list of what they wanted and needed from their bridesmaids: "I expect my bridesmaids to buy a dress of their choosing in a certain color and wear nude or gold shoes on the day." Others were far more casual: "I just need them to be there for me."

The one question I had for all of the responses was, "Have you spoken to them about this – do they know that you want them to buy nude shoes or what 'being there for you' actually means?"

Communication is ~~King~~ Queen. If we know and understand a person's needs and expectations, we can work together to either fulfill them or manage them.

Most problems (or at least the foundations of them) can be traced back to one thing – lack of communication.

If you are thinking something like 'I wish my fellow Maidchillas would help me out planning the bachelorette' but you don't communicate it to them, then, unless they have psychic abilities, it will be impossible for them to know what you actually want. This lack of communication can be frustrating for everyone, as you might be shitty that they aren't helping and they might be confused as to why you are shitty and wonder why you haven't replied to their messages even though they know you've seen them. ✔✔ They ask their friends, who have absolutely no idea what is going on, for advice and it turns into a 'thing' when it should have been a simple conversation. This is how World War II started...fact.**

I wrote this book as a companion to my two other books, *The Bridechilla Survival Guide* and *The Bridechilla Field Guide*. I hope it helps you get your shit together and ensures above all that your friendship grows during this time of potential stress and mania. Hopefully your Bridechilla friend has already read my other books, so mania will not ensue in the first place. If not, buy them as a present for her! Use the codeword MAIDCHILLA and get 15% off!

In this book I have created checklists, questions, and ideas to help you survive and thrive throughout this journey. Whether your friend wants you to 'just be there' for them or they're hoping for the full-service bridal party experience, I know you will find value and support in these pages.

Good luck my friend and Happy Days.

Aleisha

 *Honestly, spending more than 23 seconds on some of those forums makes me want to go off-grid and live on a farm with only puppies and Netflix (of course there'll be WiFi).

**Not a fact. The Second World War was started by Germany when they launched an unprovoked attack on Poland. Britain and France declared war on Germany after Hitler refused to abort his invasion. That's a fact.

NOTES

This is by far your worst idea ever...I'll be there in 15 minutes.

Anonymous

What Is a Bridechilla?

PLANNING A WEDDING CAN BE FUN, challenging, empowering, joyous, *and* a complete headfuck.

Seriously. It can bring out the best and worst in people.

Sure, it's about love; two people finding their fellow weirdos and uniting to celebrate that love in front of their family and friends. However, due to societal pressure and Pinterest, weddings have evolved into the 'event of a lifetime', where couples feel obligated to spend crazy amounts of coin on a six-hour party. With each passing year the wedding industry adds new pre-wedding events and must-have elements to the list – which can push some couples (and their budget) to screaming point.

There are so many organizational facets involved in wedding planning, both aesthetic and emotional, that it is very easy for the pressure (that I call 'wedstress') to overwhelm couples and cause issues within relationships, particularly when it comes to money and obligation.

The Bridechilla Podcast, blog, and community is all about empowerment and helping couples plan their wedding without losing their marbles in the process. It's about blocking out all of the white noise and pressure, calming the 'inspiration' overload, and really focusing on what matters most.

We spend so much time focused on the aesthetics of a wedding, when in reality most of the real stresses of wedding planning come from logistical issues such as how to integrate family, how to talk about money, and how to suppress unrealistic expectations. Wedding magazines and blogs can be helpful for all of the practical planning advice, but there isn't much chatter about the meaty stuff.

As a 'virtual bridesmaid', I have had the privilege of being able to offer Bridechillas the kind of advice that close friends and family members are reluctant to give. Often after receiving my advice, Bridechillas respond with, "I needed to hear that," or, "My mom has been telling me that for months but it wasn't until you said it that it hit home." I get it! To help get you in the Maidchilla zone, here are the basics of being a Bridechilla.

- It's about staying present and positive while saying, "Fuck it" to the shouldas, couldas and wouldas.
- It's about remembering that no matter what your budget is or your circumstances are, in the end you are planning a party celebrating that you have found your fellow weirdo.
- It's about understanding how you feel, knowing what you want, and learning how to communicate it.
- It's about listening to the voice that guides your everyday choices.
- It's about ditching obligation and not doing things just because everyone else does them.
- It's about realizing that there are plenty of things (both physical and emotional) that can be thrown in the fuck it bucket; that in the end some things will not make one ounce of difference to the outcome of the wedding.
- It's about not striving to plan a 'perfect day', because perfection doesn't exist.

Being a Maidchilla to your Bridechilla friend is about supporting each other, listening to each other, and remembering that this period is but one dot on your friendship timeline. Throughout any moments of potential stress, remember that your history is far more important than a shoe or a party. Yes, things can potentially become more challenging with new voices in the mix (I'll get to that soon), but ultimately, being invited to be a part of your friend's wedding should be an exciting time in your lives and not a ticket to Shittown.

HELPING YOUR BRIDECHILLA FRIEND DITCH WEDSTRESS

As a Maidchilla, I have watched my Bridechilla friends panic and become completely overwhelmed with the process of wedding planning – from the financial side to the notion that they have to strive for perfection (which does not exist). With exposure over the years to thousands of stories from real Bridechillas, I've heard many a tale of friendship woe. The key themes frequently featured in these breakdowns are lack of communication, emotions like jealousy and competitiveness, and finances. When money gets involved, it can drag up issues that are not connected to weddings at all.

I'm not saying that it will always be a smooth ride (Hey, that's friendship, right?), but if everyone is informed and feels like they know what they need to do and what is required of them, it will make any misunderstanding so much easier to handle.

Knowledge cannot replace friendship. I'd rather be an idiot than lose you.

Patrick to SpongeBob

So, What Does a Maidchilla Actually Do?

And is every bridesmaid the same?

IN YE OLDEN TIMES, a large group of bridesmaids provided the opportunity to show off the bride's family's social status and wealth – the more you had, the higher up the ladder you were. But the bridesmaid tradition itself originated from Roman law, which required ten witnesses at a wedding in order to outsmart evil spirits believed to attend the marriage ceremony (otherwise known as the mother-in-law! Boom-tish! Sorry). The brides-maids and ushers dressed in identical clothing to the bride and groom, so that the evil spirits wouldn't know who was getting married. So the whole thing has a bit of history...and woo-woo.

WHY DO WE HAVE BRIDESMAIDS NOWADAYS?

Many of our modern wedding rituals are based on these kinds of traditions, superstitions, and social oddities. When you break them down, they are fairly old school. Unless your Bridechilla friend is part of the Kardashian clan, they're probably not fo-cused on the symbolism and social hierarchy of the bridal party, but rather on the wedding-ruining evil spirit that is tequila.

I believe bridesmaids have been getting a bum rap recently. When did these close friends go from ladies who turn up to the church on the day in a nice dress (exactly what our mother's bridesmaids would have done) to pre-wedding slave? Bridesmaids today can sometimes be employed as emotional punching bags who organize everything from strippers to destination getaways. They are people who can be expected to go into debt to pay for a dress and talk the bride off a ledge when the napkins she ordered are delivered without the lacy imprint.

I am hoping your Bridechilla friend isn't that kind of bride (of course she isn't, she's a Bridechilla), but the evolution of the bridesmaid has been swift and I think rather brutal.

The goal of this book is to increase your enjoyment of the planning process and help make things easier for you. I want to help you get you into the Maidchilla mindset; let any drama wash over you and feel comfortable knowing you are a great friend.

Maidchillas are people who Bridechillas and Groomchillas can rely upon to help them out, plan a super awesome bachelor and bachelorette party (if that's their style), and placate any wedstress.

HOW MANY OF US WILL THERE BE?

Today, the number of bridesmaids in a wedding party depends on many variables. These range from the bride asking all twelve of her 'best friends' because she doesn't want to hurt their feelings, to the bride (fueled by four champagnes) over-enthusiastically offering a friend a place on Team Bridesmaid and then regretting it the next day, to one of my favorites, when the number of bridesmaids hinges on how many close friends the groom has so the bridal party doesn't look unbalanced!

Obligation is a big topic in Bridechilla-land, particularly how to ditch it and how to avoid the pressure of feeling like you have to do something because you feel like you should. Chances are, the number of bridesmaids is going to depend on how obligated the bride feels, and who she feels obligated to.

No matter whether the bridal party is an extended posse or a duo, working together to communicate and support your Bridechilla friend should be the collective goal. And since you are a Maidchilla, of course you are going to kick ass.

WHY DO CHICKS SEEM TO HAVE TO DO MORE WEDDING RELATED STUFF?

The gender imbalance of wedding planning is clearest to me when it comes to bridesmaids and groomsmen.

Maidchillas are lumped with a lot more shit to handle than the guys. The only things the guys are expected to do is plan a bachelor party, go to a suit fitting (which from my experience is often organized by the Bridechilla), and make sure they set an alarm on the morning of the wedding.

Wedding press, media, and blogs are also great at coming up with new ways to add to this pressure specifically for Maidchillas (WHY NOT THE DUDES?!). Extravagant Instagramable pre-wedding holidays, week-long bachelorette and hens events, bridal showers and rehearsals that are beyond any party I have ever been to... These luxurious extras are being normalized to the point that it places immense pressure on Bridechillas and Maidchillas to organize a series of pre-wedding spectaculars that a lot of people can't afford in regards to both time and money.

Although I don't want this section to be a lengthy rant about yet another gender imbalance in the wedding industry, researching this book has reaffirmed my belief that the Wedding Illuminati (the 'wedding industry') has found a consumer sweet spot in making women feel like they need all of these extra events.

Don't believe the hype. If your Bridechilla friend isn't into all these additions, ditch them or tweak them to suit you and your budget.

Weddings are a team effort – they aren't about one person planning the whole event. I'm all about challenging the old-school gendered clichés and ditching the idea that weddings are the 'lady's Super Bowl' and that the men just show up. It's bullshit and we know it.

SOME THINGS YOU MAY BE ASKED TO DO

- Help organize pre-wedding events like the bachelorette and hens celebrations, bridal shower, etc.
- Accompany your Bridechilla friend in their search for a dress, pantsuit, and/or tutu.
- Buy a dress/outfit for the day (depending on cultural expectations, you may be required to pay for said outfit).
- Give a speech at the wedding and/or rehearsal dinner.
- Be there for your friend.

LIFE IS BUSY, WE GET IT

If you live halfway across the country and have a busy job with minimal available vacation days then, very reasonably, you should be open to having a chat early on about what you are able to participate in. You don't want to find out last minute that your Bridechilla friend expects that her 30 closest friends to take off on an all-inclusive vacay to Cancun for two weeks to celebrate her bachelorette.

I know this goes against every wedding magazine and blog out there, but here goes...

- It's perfectly reasonable to be unavailable due to other commitments like work and family...and life.

- It's perfectly reasonable, albeit sucky, to be broke (I have been there).
- It's perfectly reasonable to want to go on a vacation that you have planned and not have to commit to go on a holiday with a bunch of gals if that doesn't float your boat.
- It's perfectly reasonable to be open and honest about all of the points above with your Bridechilla, because you are friends and that's what friends do.

You do you, my friend, however whatever you do, make sure you communicate. Keep the dialogue open. Chat it out. Be honest.

I implore you, as I do Bridechillas, to start a conversation early with your Bridechilla friend about their expectations, needs, and wants for your role in the wedding and the events surrounding it. The same goes for your fellow Maidchillas. Perhaps other members of the bridal party are super interested in party planning and you are better with logistics. If you know what you're all good at and in what ways you are keen to contribute, it can make it much easier at crunch time.

Calming Phrases and Things to Do for Your Bridechilla Friend When Shit Hits the Fan

Sometimes when things become pent up or a person feels like they aren't getting the support they need or want, they can act out, become emotional, or go underground. Here are some phrases and questions that can help resolve things.

- Let's see if we can solve this problem together.
- Tell me the worst thing that could possibly happen.
- It's okay to feel this way.
- What do you need from me?
- Tell me about it.
- Try to breathe.
- This feeling will pass.
- We are an unstoppable team. Let's work together!
- Let's put your worry on pause while we _____
  (watch some *Real Housewives*/drink wine/do a Zumba class/
  talk about someone's bad hair extensions/watch Dr Pimple
  Popper videos). Then we'll pick it back up again.
- I know this is hard/stressful/challenging/emotional.
- You are not alone in how you feel.
- What is the first thing we need to worry about? (This is help-
  ful if she is feeling overwhelmed by too many tasks or wor-
  ries.)
- Remember when you made it through _____.
- I get scared/nervous/anxious sometimes too. It's no fun.
- I am with you.
- We're going for a walk.
- How about a hug, then some #DogsOfInstagram videos.

A BIG LIST OF QUESTIONS TO ASK YOUR BRIDECHILLA

☐ Does the Bridechilla want to have a bachelorette party?

☐ If she isn't into a full-on booze-fest extravaganza, what would she like instead (if anything)?

☐ Who is organizing what?

☐ Does the Bridechilla want to plan her own event?

☐ Will one person take the lead or will it be a group decision? (Be careful, this can get very complicated.)

☐ Will the group be paying for the Bridechilla or will she cover her own expenses?

☐ Who selects the date?

☐ What happens if some people are not available?

☐ What is the budget for the event?

☐ Who is booking the event?

☐ How will you keep track of expenses?

☐ Will one person pay for the event and everyone else pays them back? If so, how will this occur?

☐ Will there be a fund that everyone can contribute to?

☐ Does the Bridechilla want a phallic-free event (no dicks, no strippers)?

☐ Who decides who is coming to the bachelorette party/hens/ event and who will create the guest list?

☐ Are there any conditions that the Bridechilla would like you to stick to? For example, is there anyone they really don't want to be there, like mothers or mothers-in-law?

☐ Does the couple want to combine their pre-wedding celebrations and events?

NOTES

A BIG LIST OF QUESTIONS TO ASK YOUR BRIDECHILLA

BRIDAL SHOWER

☐ Does your Bridechilla want to have a bridal shower? If so, who would she like to organize it? (Sometimes this is a great opportunity to get mom and mother-in-law involved.) _____

☐ Where would she like it to be held? _____

☐ Who does she want to be there? _____

☐ What kind of theme would she like? _____

☐ What would she like to experience? _____

☐ Would she rather an evening or weekend shower? _____

☐ Would she want guys there or would she want to make it exclusively a ladies thing? _____

☐ What kind of gifts would you like to offer? _____

☐ Does the Bridechilla want to create a shower registry? _____

☐ Are there any other pre-wedding events on her list? _____

SPEECHES

☐ Who is required to make a speech at the wedding or pre-wedding events? _____

☐ How long should the speech be? _____

☐ Is there anyone special that the Bridechilla would like the Maidchilla to acknowledge in the speech? (Sometimes Maidchillas read 'telegrams' from people that are unable to attend.) _____

NOTES

A BIG LIST OF QUESTIONS TO ASK YOUR BRIDECHILLA

☐ What can your Maidchillas do to help you in the lead up to the wedding?

☐ When are the bridal party required to arrive for the wedding (e.g. 1 day/3 days/a week before)?

☐ Who should attend the rehearsal of the wedding ceremony?

☐ Will there be a rehearsal dinner?

☐ Can people bring dates?

☐ Who is booking the wedding accommodation?

☐ Who is paying for wedding accommodation? (This applies mostly for destination weddings.)

☐ Are there any post- or pre-wedding activities you would like guests to take part in?

☐ Are there any other events you would like people to attend?

CLOTHING AND ATTIRE

☐ Would you like some company on your dress/outfit search?

☐ Do you have specific dates in mind?

☐ Do you need to pack anything specific (e.g. getting ready robes, extra shoes, iron, etc)?

MAIDCHILLA CLOTHING AND ATTIRE

☐ Is there a dress code for additional events?

☐ Do Maidchillas need to bring anything specific?

NOTES

Friends are people who know you really well and like you anyway.

Greg Tamblyn

Worlds Collide

Enforced socialization and making new friends.

YOU MAY BE ENTERING a George Costanza 'worlds collide' situation*, one in which a Bridechilla may bring together important people from all facets of her life and expect them to get along and work together, despite them being near or total strangers.

Perhaps you have known your Bridechilla friend since you were 5, or maybe you met in the office last year and just clicked, knowing that you would be instant life-long friends. Either way, you may be joining other friends in the bridal party who most definitely have their own history of how they know each other too.

The coming together of the bridal party, especially when you may not know the other people as well as your Bridechilla friend, can be challenging. It can sometimes create an odd competitive dynamic that is completely unnecessary, giving some of us flashbacks to high school. Meeting these new people can sometimes bring out insecurities in ourselves and in our friendships and make us ask questions like:

- Who is this person and why do they think they are better friends with *my* friend than I am?

- Why do they have funny anecdotes about a camping trip I have never heard of?
- Why is this shit bothering me when I am a full-grown adult with proper adult problems like finding a competitive rate for home and contents insurance?

BEING A MAIDCHILLA IS NOT ABOUT COMPETITION

Over the years I have seen some crazy shit go down with bridesmaids, incidents that make the movie *Bridesmaids* look like a documentary. Relationships need to be nurtured to flourish, and they evolve over time. People change; circumstances change. We grow both physically and emotionally and it can be really challenging to combine all of these sub-communities together. Just because you are connected by one person doesn't mean that everyone will get along or connect without any effort.

WHAT IF I REALLY DON'T VIBE WITH MY FELLOW BRIDESMAIDS?

At the age of 37, I have come to the realization that I don't have to be friends with everyone I meet. In fact, I am aware that I don't like a lot of people – not because I am an asshole, I'm really very nice. (Although isn't that what assholes say?!) I just have a low tolerance of idiots and people I have nothing in common with.

There are lots of situations in my life when I come across these people and I am quite good at being kind and friendly and gracious. But I have also reached the stage in my life when I realize that we will not always be hanging out on the weekend or catching up after work. There is precious little time and too many murder documentaries to watch to commit to people who are 'outer' friends. That's not to say we can't be friendly;

we can be associates, we can be friends of friends, or people I worked with once with whom I shared a mutual disdain for another colleague and ate lunch with every now and then. We just don't all have to be besties or pretend that the relationship is going to be anything more than it is.

WHAT TO DO IF YOU DON'T FEEL ENTIRELY POSITIVE ABOUT THE SITUATION

If you do find yourself in a 'worlds collide' situation, you don't have to be BFFs with your fellow Maidchillas, you've just got to focus on what is important – helping your Bridechilla friend maintain her chill, feel supported, and enjoy the process. Treat it like you are a contestant on *Survivor*.** Your fellow Maidchillas may end up on the jury, so you want to keep them sweet because you want that money (friendship), even if in your confessionals to the audience (your other friends, partner or co-workers) you may admit you find it annoying when they shorten words unnecessarily in WhatsApp messages and it enrages you that they have given your friend a weird nickname that only they know the origins of.

Also, just like in *Survivor*, be careful who you share information with. Be mindful that gaining and keeping someone's trust is an honor that should not be taken lightly. Different people will have different approaches to private conversations – try and be aware of whether they will share what you said in confidence to someone else.

For example, if you told Maidchilla 2 that Maidchilla 1 is a bit needy because she wanted to move the bachelorette weekend so it doesn't conflict with her new boyfriend's birthday, and then Maidchilla 2 shared that information with Maidchilla 1, what you thought was a casual comment might turn into a saga.

Sure, say what you want, be strong and confident, but be

mindful of group dynamics and of course, if things get at all hairy, outwit, outplay, and outlast.

Remember, Maidchillas are an alliance: stick together. Work together and you will win.

But I'm hoping you do connect and make friends with your fellow bridesmaids because life is better with friends.

* I really like *Seinfeld*.
** I also really like *Survivor*.

NOTES

It's the friends you can call up at 4 am that matter.

Marlene Dietrich

How Will You Communicate? Send a Raven?

ONE TEAM, ONE DREAM...which means one primary mode of group communication.

Look, I'll be honest, I communicate with different friends using different apps and sometimes it can be confusing and I end up looking like a dick because I haven't replied when really the freaking app hasn't updated and isn't sending me notifications; COME ON TECHNOLOGY YOU ARE MAKING ME LOOK LIKE A JERK.

Saying that, I think it's really good to establish a group chat situation early and make sure all of your communications are in one place. That way, it's easy to search for details and no one can say 'I didn't get that message' when we all know you did because it's sent us a double blue tick 'Jane read this' notification. ✔✔ Get with the program Jane.

MESSAGING OPTIONS

- WhatsApp.
- Viber.
- A private Facebook group, as you can create events within the group and add details such as maps and RSVPs etc.

- Group text message.
- Email chain.
- Trello board (better for collating info rather than sending messages).
- Slack.
- Some other 'young person app' that I am yet to hear about.

GIFS ARE YOUR FRIEND, AND OTHER TEXTING ETIQUETTE

GIFs are a great way to establish friendships and prevent potential misinterpretation of passive aggressiveness when it might really just be a text written in a hurry while doing a million other things (story of my life).

I find that there is a *Real Housewives* GIF for all occasions and I often use them to communicate instead of writing emails or sending emoji responses.

I also find that there is usually a dominant messenger of the group, someone who really loves to write loooooong and detailed messages. Good for them. That is not me. I am engaged but not submerged. I'll turn up to things and contribute but I won't write a message that requires you to scroll. Participation, even light participation, is better than ghosting – which is truly the worst.

NOTES

It is more fun to talk
with someone who
doesn't use long,
difficult words but
rather short,
easy words like
"What about lunch?"

A.A. Milne, *Winnie-The-Pooh*

Maidchilla Money
Who pays for what?

WE HAVE BEEN CONDITIONED TO BELIEVE that money is just not something we should talk about, but if we did talk about it, things would be *much* easier.

In my experiences as a bridesmaid before I started Bridechilla, I was challenged by conversations about money. How were we supposed to talk about who was paying for what and what our expectations were when it came to being a part of the bridal party?

The role of the bridal party has evolved past just turning up on the morning of the wedding in a nice frock or suit. It has become a year-long commitment with multiple events and activities along the way. It is fun and exciting, but it can also be problematic when you are unsure of how much money you will need to spend, and how much time you will need to take off work for travel and holidays.

Being open and communicative about money – who is paying for what and acknowledging our own financial limits – can take the heat off everyone.

NOT EVERYONE HAS THE SAME AMOUNT OF MONEY OR FINAN-CIAL PRIORITIES

As a freelancer and creative person, I am often broke. When surrounded by people with 'real jobs' it can sometimes suck to have to admit to myself and them that I can't always afford to be spontaneous and footloose with my money. We are all in different financial situations and I am constantly reminding Bridechillas that there shouldn't be shame attached to money. Shit happens, financial circumstances change, but ultimately it is about surrounding yourself with people who care for you and want to share memories with you of this special time in your life.

There has been a ridiculous boom of pre-wedding events that end up being bigger than the actual wedding. International travel, week-long holidays, and meals in private rooms at Michelin-starred restaurants have become the norm in the lead up to the event itself. I read about them and I ask myself, "Who the fuck are these people and where did they get the money and time off work to do this stuff?"

Granted, a lot of them are probably 'Instagram Influencers' and robots for all I know, but, like a lot of shit connected to the wedding industry, the media raises everyone's expectations and normalizes these experiences and spending.

BEING HONEST ABOUT MONEY CAN BE HARD, BUT IT IS WORTH IT

If you aren't in the situation to pay for events or expensive dresses and extras – if you will be forced to go into debt for these things – then I implore you to speak to your Bridechilla friend.

There is no shame in being unable to afford something or get time off work or use vacation days you don't have. It doesn't mean you are not a good friend – in fact I think being honest shows your friend just how much you mean to each other.

- Friends listen to friends.
- Friends aren't shitty towards friends because circumstances change.
- Friends, even when it's tough, are honest with friends.
- *Friends* was a TV show from the 2000s.

THE BIG LIST OF THINGS YOU MIGHT WANT TO BUY

Your Maidchilla budget:

DRESSES & ATTIRE · · · · ·	BUDGETED	SPENT
Shoes		
Jewelery		
Underwear		
Dress		
Hair accessories		
Hair stylist		
Makeup		
Makeup artist		
Total:		

ACCOMMODATION · · · · ·	BUDGETED	SPENT
Bachelorette/Hens		
Bridal shower		
Post-wedding brunch		
Total:		

NOTES

THE BIG LIST OF THINGS YOU MIGHT WANT TO BUY

Your Maidchilla budget:

OTHER · · · · · · · · ·	BUDGETED	SPENT

Total:	

NOTES

THE BIG LIST OF THINGS YOU MIGHT WANT TO BUY

Your Maidchilla budget:

OTHER · · · · · · · · ·	BUDGETED	SPENT
Total:		

NOTES

You and I are more than friends. We're like a really small gang.

Anonymous

Maidchilla Attire

Frocking up with the flock.

T‍HE DECISION OF WHAT TO WEAR on your Bridechilla friend's wedding day may be yours, or perhaps it will be solely theirs. Being dressed by someone else is weird. "But it's tradition!" I hear people exclaim. It may well be tradition, but for many Bridechillas this tradition is evolving. The trend of matching dresses is becoming less popular and the selection of attire has become a more egalitarian affair.

The current trend of mismatched Maidchillas is awesome. It's an ideal solution to the dilemma of catering to different body shapes and a lovely way to personalize attire while still sticking to a theme or color scheme. Bridechillas can, for example, select a color/length/designer and open it up to you to choose your own dresses or outfit within that criteria. Or, if they are having the dresses made, they may choose the material and give you the option of selecting a style of dress that suits you.

I love this option as it enables you to have the chance to select a style that you are comfortable in, that flatters your body, and that makes you feel fabulous!

There are plenty of websites that offer a wide range of simple formal gowns, dresses and jumpsuits (!) specifically designed to be customized. They also offer swatches so you can purchase the same color dresses in different sizes and cuts. If you are ordering online, allow at least two months for shipping, alterations, and returns if necessary.

I spoke with a Bridechilla recently who said that she had placed a large order with Asos. She chose a big selection of styles, sizes, and colors for her Maidchillas. They then made a day of it, trying on the dresses and deciding together what they liked. After the decision was made they simply sent back all the unwanted dresses and got a refund. I think this was a lovely idea that allowed the group to bond and sample some dresses without having to leave the house! There are many online stores offering similar services in a variety of budget ranges, so this is a great option, particularly if trekking around stores doesn't float your boat.

Another terrific option is renting your Maidchilla outfits from a company like Rent the Runway. It's extremely affordable, you can use coupon codes to get discounts, and you can all try on the dresses before the big day. And again, you can rent multiple dresses to see what suits you the most.

These companies have a huge selection of high-end designer clothes that would be pretty pricey to purchase for the day, but can be rented for a song. You can often get a good deal if you hire more than one dress, which means adding rehearsal dinner attire or after-party dresses to your rental can make for very good value.

For my wedding I wasn't interested in the typical bridesmaid get up. I asked my Maidchillas to wear their favorite little black dress, and I found some gorgeous patterned pashminas that I gave them as a gift. The coordinated scarves really tied the looks together without putting the bridal party under any additional financial pressure. They loved what they wore because they chose it – and they could wear it again.

In my home country of Australia, Maidchilla dresses are usually funded by the couple, whereas I know many Bridechillas in the USA ask their Maidchillas to pay for their own dresses.

I encourage you, as a Maidchilla, to ask questions and seek out conversations if your Bridechilla hasn't given you enough information. Get them to be open with you about their expectations of your attire and your financial input. Talking about money is never easy, but if everyone is on the same page there will be no need for any animosity or potential weirdness.

As a Maidchilla you might say, "Hey lady, if you want me to wear that taffeta monstrosity that moonlights as a bedspread then you pay for it." Your Bridechilla friend may say, "Hey, I've held your hair while you vomited and I never acknowledge that your fake tan is too dark, give it up and buy the goddamn dress that I want. I'd do it for you."

Having been a Maidchilla and a Bridechilla, I will say both parties are right. But I think it's important to discuss who's paying for what before making any decisions.

If the bridal party is paying for the dress/suit, then a discussion of budget is necessary. Not everyone has $400+ to spend on a cocktail dress and shoes. If it's awkward for you to talk about this with the group, then speak with your Bridechilla friend privately.

If it's between you paying your rent or buying a gown, then take that into consideration – for the sake of your friendship and having a roof over your head!

I DON'T WANT TO WEAR THAT – MAIDCHILLA ATTIRE

Some people are more confident and more outspoken than others. Some people can be pushy. Some people can be defensive when they are challenged to do something (or wear something) that might not be their style.

When considering outfits and combinations for the bridal party, I am hoping that your Bridechilla friend and your fellow Maidchillas will consider the diversity of the group and your different body shapes and sizes. Who will be comfortable in what, and is there a possibility of the attendants being able to wear their dress or suit in the future? How wonderful would it be for you to enjoy wearing your chosen wedding outfit again instead of it hanging in your wardrobe for the next five years. I am sure that bridal parties would happily pay for the outfit if they think they will be able to wear and enjoy it again.

That said, sometimes your Bridechilla friend's sense of style and your sense of style are very different, and that is okay. Sometimes, for the sake of your friend's happiness and vision, it's best to just suck it up and wear the dress (unless you really, *really* feel opposed to it).

If you do have reservations, speak privately and calmly to your friend. Don't be brash in a group chat; don't pout or be a jerk. Think about how you would want someone to share their opinion about a choice that was important to you. Take a moment and breathe. Be kind, be calm, and if in doubt, have a vodka soda.

NOTES

Best Wedding Movies

A night on the couch with friends, snacks, and a glass of wine (or four) may be just what the doctor ordered. Flick on one of these wedding movies and you will be right in the zone.

FUNNY & LOVEY-DOVEY

Bridesmaids
Muriel's Wedding
Wedding Crashers
The Hangover
Father Of the Bride (1950 version and Steve Martin version)
Four Weddings and a Funeral
The Princess Bride
My Big Fat Greek Wedding
Runaway Bride
My Best Friend's Wedding
The Wedding Singer
American Wedding

27 Dresses
Mamma Mia!
I Love You, Man
The Proposal
Sex and the City
Meet the Parents
Three Men and a Little Lady
The Wedding Planner
The Wedding Date
Bride Wars
Monster-in-Law
The Sweetest Thing
Love Actually
Meet the Fockers

INTENSE AND ARTY

Melancholia
The Corpse Bride
The Wedding Banquet
Monsoon Wedding

CLASSICS

Royal Wedding
The Graduate
The Philadelphia Story
It's a Wonderful Life

NOTES

Two people are never such good friends as when they share a mutual dislike of a third person.

Anonymous

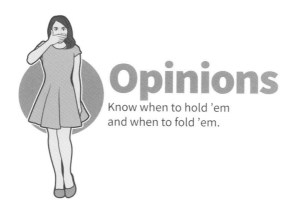

Opinions

Know when to hold 'em
and when to fold 'em.

AS THE WISE SAYING GOES, "Opinions are like assholes; everyone's got one."

Everyone has something to say, and no matter how helpful they think they are, people can be damn frustrating. This is especially prevalent when you are in a group situation where people are feeling each other out and may or may not be experiencing underlying competitiveness and silliness.

The opinion-givers believe that by telling you just how much their idea is worth considering you will suddenly change your plans or realize what a genius they are, even when you are confident with your choices. Sometimes people offer opinions because they truly believe they know better than you, but other times it can come back to the fear of not being heard, or just plain old insecurity.

In a group environment like a bunch of Maidchillas meeting up to pick dresses, you often see one of two things:

- Everyone has an opinion, or
- No one wants to step up and give their opinion out of fear of being wrong, not wanting to be in charge, being too busy, or out of sheer laziness.

There will always be one member of a group who thinks that they know best (and sometimes, although very rarely, they do).

Perhaps they have just gotten married (or they're engaged) and therefore, of course, they have become the unofficial and self-proclaimed oracle of weddings. Maybe their sister's friend's work colleague just got hitched and they heard ALL about it and don't want you to 'make the same mistakes as them'.

It can be annoying to hear these comparisons, or to feel like your supposed inexperience as a Maidchilla means that you are less qualified to share your opinions. It can be challenging working with people who, due to their own insecurities about being in a group, feel the need to speak up about everything.

IS IT WORTH THE ARGUMENT?

Personally, these are the people I have to take a step back from and ask myself, "Is it worth my energy getting shitty?" and, "What will I gain by putting Brenda back in her place when she spouts misinformation about wedding traditions that she read about in a 2003 edition of *The Knot* at the dermatologist's office last week?"

I am the person who wants to take Brenda and her big mouth down. But I know that Brenda is my Bridechilla friend's friend, and putting Brenda in a headlock could affect the Bridechilla's enjoyment of the Maidchilla experience and make me look like a psycho.

If there are personalities in the bridal party (and extended family) that you find difficult, then I encourage you to step back, breathe, and avoid sending texts or messages that could be misinterpreted (or indeed interpreted correctly!).

When thinking about know-it-alls and people that annoy me, I am reminded of my Grandmother Mary and a favorite saying of hers, "Never argue with an idiot. They will only bring you down to their level and beat you with experience."

So how do you deal with unwanted opinions or nosiness without being a jerk?

One of my favorite opinion-slaying sayings comes from Oprah, OF COURSE! I love it because it demonstrates how relatable and bloody great that lady is, but the simplicity and power of the phrase also has a tinge of finality about it without being too rude. Are you ready?

"That's not going to work for me."

What I love about this saying is that it is direct but polite. The opinion-giver doesn't have much opportunity to reply. If you want to soften the blow, you can add, "Thanks so much for thinking of me/us. That's a good idea, but it's not going to work for me/us." That way their opinion has been heard, but they aren't under the impression that you are going to change your plans or follow their course of action just because they suggested it. Sharing opinions can be a delicate and complicated balance of not offending people while still being strong enough to use your voice.

Focus on working as a team with your Maidchilla group – make decisions together and avoid being strong-armed into doing something just because one member of the group is louder or pushier than the rest. It isn't always easy and requires resilience and commitment to the cause, but trust me when I say it will be worth it.

PEOPLE DO THINGS DIFFERENTLY

If you are also getting married (hurrah!) and are doing things differently than your Bridechilla friend, that is A-OK.

One of the most challenging topics I have seen discussed in the Bridechilla Community is Bridechillas clashing with engaged (or newly married) Maidchillas over the different ways that they are choosing to plan and celebrate their wedding.

Your wedding (should you have one), and your Bridechilla friend's wedding will no doubt be very different and fabulous in their own ways. I am sure your choices surrounding your planning, taste, budget, families, and overall vision will differ from that of your Bridechilla friend's. I encourage you, when you think you may be heading down the path to comparison, to pause a moment. Just because you may be doing things differently doesn't mean one way is right and the other way is wrong; one way is the right way for you and another way may be right for your Bridechilla friend. Don't fall into the trap of letting different paths get in the way of helping each other.

NOTES

Lots of people want to ride with you in the limo, but what you want is someone who will take the bus with you when the limo breaks down.

Oprah Winfrey

Don't Go Changing... Or Do...

HERE'S THE THING. People cut their hair, get preggo, find new partners or end relationships. That is life, my friends. I have heard some pretty bizarre accounts of arguments (and friendship deaths) that stem from a bridesmaid changing her hair before the wedding and the bride freaking out about it (note that I didn't say Bridechilla!).

Sure, if you're planning on getting a buzz cut or going St Patrick's Day green a week before the wedding, it could present a challenging situation for your Bridechilla friend. In those cases I would suggest being mindful and communicative about what you are planning to do. I'm not saying you shouldn't cut your hair or make changes, but if you're planning something dramatic, let the bride know in advance. That way you can avoid unnecessary conflict, or the hassle of buying a last minute hat or wig.

PREGNANCY ≠ BAD BRIDESMAID

Pregnancy is something that happens every day. People make people and they aren't going to stop making people because someone else is getting hitched. If you're pregnant and a bridesmaid, I'm guessing you've probably shared the news with your Bridechilla friend. Work together to look at attire options and consider what you think you may be able to manage when it comes to pre-wedding celebrations.

Pregnancy is not an illness – pregnant women rock – but know your limits and don't be shy about asking for help and a sensible shoe. If the pre-wedding pace is too hectic, tell your friend and you can work together to make it more comfortable so you don't miss out.

BREAKUPS AND HEARTBREAK

Partners can come and go, but friendships hopefully follow the seasons of life. I have been a bridesmaid during the peak of a pretty devastating relationship breakdown and I'm going to be honest with you, it wasn't all sunshine and roses. I was so happy for my friend. Genuinely, wholeheartedly happy.

But I was also sad for me and confused as to what the hell I was going to do with the rest of my life. I wondered if I would ever meet a decent bloke again. I tried so hard to bury that shit down deep and be a supportive friend, and I think I did a good job.

We have phases of our lives that are great and phases that are not so great. Finding the balance of being supportive and genuine while being mindful of your own heath and well-being is really important. You don't have to feign happiness, but making a good go at having a nice time and allowing yourself to be involved in the revelry can be a positive step.

Like all of my advice, be open about your feelings. By this I don't mean drink a bottle of gin at the bachelorette party and sabotage the evening with a black out meltdown about how you will be alone for ever...ahem...Instead share how you are feeling with your Bridechilla friend. If you are finding certain aspects of the planning process or social situations difficult to navigate, then arrange a time to speak with your Bridechilla friend and let them know how you feel.

Pick your moment.

Be open.

Be kind.

The true heart of friendship is weathering life together, and supporting each other through the good times and the shit times.

Some people
go to priests;
others to poetry;
I to my friends.

Virginia Woolf

Wedstress

How to help your Bridechilla
friend and help yourself.

OF ALL OF THE THINGS TO GET STRESSED ABOUT, a party is not something I imagine a modern woman would place high on the list. But wedstress is real, and it can cause real issues for some couples. Beyond planning bachelorette parties and trying on a thousand dresses, the real role of a Maidchilla is to provide support and encouragement when the potential insanity of wedding planning really kicks in.

YOU ARE A GREAT FRIEND

You have been selected to be a part of the bridal party, and I am hoping that's because you are a great and supportive friend. You have funny stories, embarrassing moments, and shared highs and lows in the friendship back catalogue. These are experiences that will far exceed any minor dramas of planning a wedding, but in the lead up to the event things can get pretty intense. People deal with stress in different ways, and that will probably become more apparent the closer you get to the day.

SHOWING KINDNESS AND UNDERSTANDING = FUCKING GREAT FRIEND

Being mindful of anxiety, mental health, and physical health is something that wedding magazines and pretty blogs don't always focus on. But it is a shame they don't, because these factors that are so important in our daily lives can become exaggerated during wedding planning.

We can't switch off mental health issues just because we are involved in wedding planning. People get sick, accidents happen, people lose their jobs, people gain weight, people lose weight, grandparents die, people move, people buy houses, people sell houses, people make money, people lose money, people study, people work two jobs, people fall in love, people break up...you get it. All of this shit continues to happen no matter what event is on the horizon.

Coping with all of these situations can be challenging, but, as I advise the Bridechilla Community, when 'life happens' you need to take a moment, breathe, and formulate a plan. We can deal with anything when we have love and support – something I know you can bring and do!

LOOK AFTER YOURSELF AND YOUR BRIDECHILLA FRIEND

I advise all of my Bridechilla readers and listeners that beyond any detail of wedding planning, it's very important to look after yourself. If that means excusing yourself for an event, or taking a step back from planning, make sure you step up and do what's best for you, your friend and your friendship.

Maidchillas are the unsung heroes of weddings. I know it's not always easy and sometimes it can even feel a little thankless, but know that you are there because you are a very special person in the Bridechilla's life. That friendship is the most important thing, beyond any momentary desire to go into a field and scream.

Stress can make people reactive. It can make people say things and act in a way that isn't great.

Remember that.

Be kind, and, if in doubt, have a quiet moment with a crisp glass of Sauvignon Blanc and watch *Real Housewives*. That always works for me.

SOME WEDDING RELATED DE-STRESS ACTIVITIES THAT YOU CAN DO TOGETHER...OR ALONE

- Move your body.
- Try a new exercise class.
- Go swimming.
- Do some yoga or pilates.
- Walk with a good podcast and just space out.
- Go to a high tea, eat scones with a lot of cream, and drink tea/champs.
- Spend a whole day inside bingeing on a new TV series.
- Do a cross-stitch.
- Play with a puppy, and if you don't have access to one, do what my husband Rich and I do and go to a dog park!

Sometimes me think, "What is friend?" Then me say, "Friend is someone to share last cookie with."

Cookie Monster

The Bridal Shower

THE BRIDAL SHOWER IS A PRE-WEDDING PARTY for the couple to set up their new home. It comes from the ancient past where people didn't shack up together before the wedding and when getting married was the first occasion that the couple lived together. The gifts were generally homewares – kitchen items, linens etc. – and the guests were only women because of course we were the ones who belonged in the kitchen and made the beds! Sarcasm aside, the bridal shower does not have to be a salute to the patriarchy like it was before.

Nowadays, the bridal shower is frequently a tradition that the older folk ask to include in the celebrations because it's 'what you do'. Very often it is a chance for the moms, aunts and grandmothers to host an event that doesn't involve dick straws and slut drops (although if a bridal shower does involve both of those, then more power to you).

THEME THE EVENT

While the themes and types of bridal showers have diversified in recent years, the general format remains the same: a daytime ladies' event in celebration of the Bridechilla's upcoming marriage. There are often kitchen related gifts (rather patriarchal, I know), shower games, cakes and champagne.

Many Bridechillas in our community ditch the bridal shower altogether, or choose to take a modern path like a couple's shower, in which the couple's friends, no matter their gender, are invited. Another popular option is to host a cellar party and invite friends to bring wine or spirits to stock the couple's home bar.

WHERE WILL THE SHOWER TAKE PLACE?

The bridal shower is often hosted by moms, aunts, grandmothers or friends and therefore can take place at a familial home or at a venue such as a hotel or even a café.

WHO SHOULD BE INVITED?

As with other pre-wedding events, the guest list should be limited to people who are also invited to the wedding. For the bridal shower, this usually includes the bridal party, the bride and groom's mothers and sisters, aunts, close female cousins, and grandmothers.

GIFTING

As a large majority of couples are already sharing a home together, I advise that you speak with your Bridechilla friend and ask for advice about what sort of gifts (if any) they would like to receive. Many online registry companies offer the option to register for bridal shower gifts also, and if there is a specific gift that the couple would find helpful, like a great chef's knife or a steam cleaner (I could watch those videos all day) this could be an ideal opportunity for guests to chip in and gift something that is useful and needed, rather than just purchasing a bunch of stuff that may or may not make it to the kitchen bench. Cookbooks are a great gift and creating your own cookbook using your guests' favorite recipes is a wonderful personalized gift too.

SHOWER THEMES

- Flower arranging class.
- Spa day.
- Self-care/spa shower – nail stations, face masks and massages.
- Film-inspired.
- Recipe swap.
- Garden party.
- Retro brunch.
- Fiesta.
- TV themed: *Game of Thrones*, *Dexter* (!), *Mad Men*, *Downtown Abbey*, *Westworld*, *Seinfeld* (obvs).
- Tea party.
- Tropicana.
- Slumber party.
- Ice cream insanity (I just made that up, but I envisage *everything* being ice-cream themed, and of course an ice cream stand).
- Waffle or pancake party.
- Pool party.
- Winter wonderland.
- BBQ.

BRIDAL SHOWER
GUEST LIST

NAME	ATTENDING		
	YES	NO	MAYBE
	☐	☐	☐
	☐	☐	☐
	☐	☐	☐
	☐	☐	☐
	☐	☐	☐
	☐	☐	☐
	☐	☐	☐
	☐	☐	☐
	☐	☐	☐
	☐	☐	☐
	☐	☐	☐
	☐	☐	☐
	☐	☐	☐
	☐	☐	☐
	☐	☐	☐
	☐	☐	☐
	☐	☐	☐
	☐	☐	☐
	☐	☐	☐
	☐	☐	☐

BRIDAL SHOWER
GUEST LIST

NAME	ATTENDING		
	YES	NO	MAYBE
	☐	☐	☐
	☐	☐	☐
	☐	☐	☐
	☐	☐	☐
	☐	☐	☐
	☐	☐	☐
	☐	☐	☐
	☐	☐	☐
	☐	☐	☐
	☐	☐	☐
	☐	☐	☐
	☐	☐	☐
	☐	☐	☐
	☐	☐	☐
	☐	☐	☐
	☐	☐	☐
	☐	☐	☐
	☐	☐	☐
	☐	☐	☐
	☐	☐	☐

THE BRIDAL SHOWER SHOPPING LIST

Total budget:

ITEM • • • • • • • • • • • •	BUDGET	SPENT

Total:

THE BRIDAL SHOWER
SHOPPING LIST

Total budget:

ITEM · · · · · · · · · · · ·	BUDGET	SPENT

Total:

Over-Gifting

One of my favorite things to diss are gifts. Gifts for the bridal party, gifts for the parents, gifts for the driver that drove you to the venue. I mean, we seem a little bit obsessed with giving people gifts. Don't get me wrong, I love gifts – I love receiving gifts, I love giving gifts. But at the moment, we are going through a gift-giving renaissance. And the renaissance needs to end because The Bridechilla Community is swamped with messages from Chillas saying:

I don't know what to give this person as a gift.
I feel stressed about having to find a gift.
I haven't got time to think about a gift.
Do I need to give them a gift?
How much should I spend on the gift?
When should I give them the gift?
Do I need to give them a gift to say, "Thank you for asking me to be in your bridal party?"

No! Stop it! Stop with the gifts. It stresses me out, man. Consider the gift bag. The thought is lovely, but no one's going to judge you, or think any less of you, if you don't give your Bridechilla friend a gift every couple of weeks to mark some point in the planning process. A card, or something handwritten and delightful, is perfect and much more personalized and thoughtful especially if you're on a budget. Excess gifts are in the Fuck It Bucket now. The FIB, of course, is my favorite place to put unwanted tasks, gifts, pressures, and obligations. Try it, you'll like it. Learn all about it in *The Bridechilla Survival Guide*!

A true friend is someone who thinks that you are a good egg even though he knows that you are slightly cracked.

Bernard Meltzer

Let's Get This Party Started

PART OF THE CHALLENGE in arranging a bachelorette day (or weekend...or week) is finding an activity that pleases everyone.

Well lady, you can just pack that idea up right now, because bachelorette party planning is just like life; there will always be one person who has some objection to something, or a suggestion as to how to make it better. Sometimes their suggestions are good, but sometimes you just want to throw the phone across the room because that person is the only one who doesn't want to go along with a group plan. That behavior can be both complicated and annoying, but I say, "Fuck 'em".

By now I am hoping that you, and the group, have spoken to your Bridechilla friend about what sort of activities or event she might like to have – perhaps she's even organizing it, or helping you out? Either way, decide who is doing what before you move on to the planning phase.

WHEN TO PARTY?

The bachelorette celebration is typically the final group event that happens closest to the wedding. Planning a date in advance that isn't too close to W-day is recommended. A few months before is ideal as celebrations can be enjoyed without too much hassle, hangovers, or overlap with other pre-wedding activities and organization.

Surprises are fun, but always be mindful of keeping your Bridechilla friend's personality – and wants and needs – in mind. There's no need to plan a *Hangover*-style escapade if she would prefer an activity like relaxing at an Airbnb with a pool or taking a cocktail class.

The list of ideas on page 82 can be used as a jumping off point at the beginning of discussions when inevitably someone asks in the group chat, "So, what are we doing and where are we going?" and then just disappears while you do all the work.

The list contains activities and themes for all budgets. Some require travel, and some you can make work in your own backyard, local bar, or Airbnb.

WHO IS INVITED?

Typically, bachelorette celebrations are reserved for Maidchillas and maybe a few of the Bridechilla's closest friends and female family members. Of course, this can change depending on the type of celebration you are planning and the activities you end up choosing.

Are moms, aunts and grandmas invited? If so, a dick-swinging stripper might not be appropriate (or might be *very* appropriate depending on the person!). Asking your Bridechilla friend for a guest list of people they would like to invite and their expectations about how many guests they imagined attending the celebration will be extremely helpful for you. You may have a very different party planning experience if there are five people versus fifty on the list.

If in doubt, communicate with your Bridechilla friend and

ask if certain people should be there or not. You will need to manage expectations if there are people who cannot attend.

The Bridechilla ethos isn't big on traditions, but for me there's only one real guest list no-no and that is inviting anyone who has not received an invitation to the wedding. The same goes for other events like bridal showers.

From the guest's perspective it can be awkward to be invited to the pre-wedding celebrations, perhaps even give a gift, and then get the door closed on them for the main event. Do your research and find out who is absolutely on the list and who isn't.

GET THE WORD OUT

Depending on your Bridechilla friend and their expectations (and involvement), formal invites aren't always necessary. Perhaps you have a WhatsApp or Facebook group going where you can upload all of the info. Or if you are after something pretty, I would recommend using Paperless Post. Make sure to send out invitations or information well in advance if you are planning a weekender so that guests can clear their schedules.

In the invitations/group notices, be sure to clearly convey all the information about the event. This should include:

- When the event starts/ends and transportation info.
- RSVP date and when deposits are due.
- Who to address the deposits to and how (Venmo, bank, PayPal info, etc).
- The total price of the activity/event per person.
- If accommodation isn't included, suggestions of where people can stay.
- If you have agreed that you are all splitting the Bridechilla's expenses, a final figure of how much that will be.
- Contact details of main organizer (or the RSVP collector).

WHAT ARE THE VIBES?

Whatever activity or event you choose, remember that it is about a bunch of friends – or new friends, or people that meet a few times and never see each other again – coming together in celebration of your mutual friend. Some of the best bachelorette days I have attended have been simple and fun, with good food, booze, and music.

- Be mindful of not 'over-producing' an event or trying to cram too much into a day/evening/weekend.
- Give people time to travel, mingle, and relax. Try to avoid a really tight timeline, especially when booze is involved.
- Think about budget and financial commitment. Being involved in weddings can be expensive and it can be hard for people to admit that they might not be able to afford certain things. Always be kind, and try to understand alternate perspectives and situations.
- Be mindful that your plans may not fit in with everyone else's schedule and prior commitments. Just because someone can't make it doesn't make them a shit friend.

NOTES

Bachelorette Ideas

EVENTS, CLASSES, AND PARKS

A trip to the theatre
Take a makeup class - great if you are DIY for the wedding
Comic Con
Flower arranging class
Sailing lesson
If you're near a beach, get a surf lesson
Theme parks – roller coasters, water parks, Disneyland
Escape rooms
Visit an adult ball pit
TV show taping
Music festival with glamping
Roller-skating or roller derby class
Silent disco
Make your own scented candles or perfume
Street art tour
Yoga retreat
Go to a cat café
Wedding hat making
A graffiti workshop
A chocolate crawl
Cocktails and karaoke

ADULT-THEMED

Hire a Butler in the Buff to serve drinks (they even wash up!)
Strip clubs and shows
Life painting class

BOOZE AND FOOD

Winery, craft beer, or distillery tour
Baking or cocktail class (or both!)
Bottomless brunch (look for a fabulous deal)
Host a backyard luau

STAY IN

Binge on wedding movies (check out page 50 for suggestions!)
Home spa: face masks, nail painting and tanning
Home high tea
Rent a beach house or pool house and get your cocktail on

LET'S GET PHYSICAL

Hiking and camping, quad biking, or glamping
Clay-pigeon shooting
Compete in Tough Mudder
Dancing classes: Bollywood, burlesque, Beyonce (yep)
Mobile day spa
Laser tag
Go karts
Bowling

THEMES

Summer camp: zip lining, horseback riding, kayaking
Foodie tour
Scavenger hunt
Wellness retreat: at home with DIY treatments or hire a yoga
instructor and beautician to come to you

BACHELORETTE GUEST LIST

NAME	ATTENDING		
	YES	NO	MAYBE
	☐	☐	☐
	☐	☐	☐
	☐	☐	☐
	☐	☐	☐
	☐	☐	☐
	☐	☐	☐
	☐	☐	☐
	☐	☐	☐
	☐	☐	☐
	☐	☐	☐
	☐	☐	☐
	☐	☐	☐
	☐	☐	☐
	☐	☐	☐
	☐	☐	☐
	☐	☐	☐
	☐	☐	☐
	☐	☐	☐
	☐	☐	☐
	☐	☐	☐
	☐	☐	☐
	☐	☐	☐

BACHELORETTE
GUEST LIST

NAME	ATTENDING		
	YES	NO	MAYBE
	☐	☐	☐
	☐	☐	☐
	☐	☐	☐
	☐	☐	☐
	☐	☐	☐
	☐	☐	☐
	☐	☐	☐
	☐	☐	☐
	☐	☐	☐
	☐	☐	☐
	☐	☐	☐
	☐	☐	☐
	☐	☐	☐
	☐	☐	☐
	☐	☐	☐
	☐	☐	☐
	☐	☐	☐
	☐	☐	☐
	☐	☐	☐
	☐	☐	☐

THE BACHELORETTE CELEBRATION TIMELINE

TIME	EVENT
:	
:	
:	
:	
:	
:	
:	
:	
:	
:	
:	
:	
:	
:	
:	
:	
:	
:	
:	
:	

THE BACHELORETTE
CELEBRATION TIMELINE

TIME	EVENT
:	
:	
:	
:	
:	
:	
:	
:	
:	
:	
:	
:	
:	
:	
:	
:	
:	
:	
:	
:	

THE BACHELORETTE PARTY
SHOPPING LIST

Total budget:

ITEM	BUDGET	SPENT

Total:

THE BACHELORETTE PARTY SHOPPING LIST

Total budget:

ITEM · · · · · · · · · · · · ·	BUDGET	SPENT

Total:

Non-Trad Bachelorette Party Games

NEVER HAVE I EVER...

Take turns making a personal confession, such as: "Never have I ever...returned clothes after wearing them." If someone in the group has done that thing (including the speaker), they must take a sip of their drink. If it's a particularly salacious story then share it!

TELL ME LIES... (FLEETWOOD MAC'S LITTLE LIES WOULD BE A GREAT INTRO SONG)

Who is good at lying? Who is wearing their Lady Gaga poker face? Have your guests share two pieces of personal information about themselves – one of which is a truth, and the other, a lie. Can the group guess which one is the lie? Ask as many tricky and awkward follow-up questions as you can, and see who cracks first!

PIÑATA

Fill it with goodness and smack the shit out of it. This is also terrific therapy for wedstress. You can also fill the piñata with mini alcoholic drinks instead of candy... just saying.

BRIDECHILLA BINGO

Download a free template (there are literally thousands), print it out and let the games begin.

BRIDECHILLA SCAVENGER HUNT

Scavenger hunts can be fun and challenging if well prepared. Give a checklist to each of your guests and have them race each other to find objects or take photos of certain items, situations, or people. Guests can work individually or as a team, the rules are up to you. There's a nice variety of scavenger hunts that range from the wild to the tame, so you should be able to find a hunt with the perfect balance for your group.

MAIDS CHARADES

Look, there's nothing really new about this game – I just like the name! However, if you wish to divert from the original premise of acting out a film, activity, or phrase, you could theme the actions around your Bridechilla's life and favorite things.

THE COUPLE QUIZ

This classic bachelorette party game will put your Bridechilla under the spotlight as she puts her knowledge to the test. Simply ask the Bridechilla's fiancé(e) to answer the questions beforehand, and then ask your Bridechilla friend the same questions. Once she's answered each question, compare their answers to see if she's correct. Pick 15 or so questions from the list below.

What is your favorite characteristic of your partner?
Where was your favorite date?
What article of your clothing would your partner love for you to get rid of?
What article of your partner's clothing would you like them to get rid of?
When was the first time you said "I love you?"
What is the most unusual place you've ever hooked up?
What is their worst habit?
What would they say is yours?
How many kids do you want, if any?
Who hogs the bed covers?
What is the best present your partner has given you?
What is something your partner has too much of?
What was your first impression of your partner?
When did you know you wanted to marry your partner?
Where was your first kiss?
Who said 'I love you' first?
What was the first meal they cooked for you?
What was the first meal you cooked for them?
What was the first movie you saw together?

What was the first trip you took together?
What's the best date you've ever been on?
What is their favorite animal?
What is their proudest achievement?
What is their most embarrassing moment?
If your partner could have any band or musician perform at your wedding, who would it be?
What is their favorite item of clothing?
What is their favorite city in the world?
What is your favorite part of their body?
What is their favorite part of your body?
What item of clothing does your partner look best in?
Describe their ideal date night with you.
When is your partner happiest?
What is their nickname?
What is their nickname for you?
Who is their celebrity crush?
What's your couple song?
What color eyes do they have?
What is their most annoying habit?
What would they say is your most annoying habit?
Who would you say is the boss in the relationship?
Would you trust them to choose your wedding dress?
Who is the funniest in the relationship?
Who is the tidiest?
Who is the better cook?
Who takes up the most room in bed?
Who has the best taste?
If your partner were an animal, what animal would they be?
What actors would play you in the movie of your relationship?
What would the movie of your relationship be called?

HOW WELL DO YOU KNOW YOUR BRIDECHILLA FRIEND?

This simple quiz is a fun way to kick off a bachelorette party.

When is the Bridechilla's birthday?
Who was her first kiss?
Where did the bride-to-be meet her partner?
What's the Bridechilla's drink of choice?
What's her middle name?
How many siblings does she have?
Where is the honeymoon?
What is her go-to hangover food?
Who is the Bridechilla's celebrity crush?
What's the last TV show she binge-watched?
What was the Bridechilla's first concert?
What's her biggest pet peeve?
What's the Bridechilla's shoe size?
What's the Bridechilla's dream job?
How did her partner propose?

THE BRIDECHILLA QUIZ

Perhaps the most amusing of the quiz games, this is the perfect time and vehicle to unearth all those embarrassing stories about the Bridechilla's murky past. In this game, the Bridechilla's friends contribute the quiz questions, preferably ones alluding to incidents and memories from her life. The quizmaster then collects the questions, and poses them for the group to answer, and hopefully laugh about (the person who wrote the question is not allowed to answer). Some quiz questions might even be for the Bridechilla herself. *This* is when you can draw out the funny and embarrassing stories, not at the wedding.

This game can be a great way for guests to get to know one another. Hand out the game cards as guests arrive. The goal is for them to find someone who fits the criteria below and fill in the other guest's name. The winner is the first person to finish or the person that fills in the most names in a set amount of time. To make it more fun, guests can read their answers to the group at the end. Of course, edit and change the questions depending on your guests.

You need to find someone who:

- was born the same month as you
- wears the same shoe size as you
- has the same favorite TV show as you
- has the same favorite color as you
- has been to Australia
- speaks a foreign language
- has the same favorite pizza topping as you
- didn't make their bed this morning
- is the oldest sibling in their family
- is vegan (or pretends to be)
- has been on a blind date
- has a phobia (e.g. fear of heights)
- has the same eye color as you
- has had a weird Craig's List experience
- likes Nepalese food
- has freebased cocaine*

* Jokes. Best not to ask this.

Tis the privilege of friendship to talk nonsense, and to have her nonsense respected.

Charles Lamb

Speech Making

Giving a speech at a wedding or event is a big deal, and for a lot of people, public speaking evokes feelings of extreme terror. That reminds me of this quote from Jerry Seinfeld:

> According to most studies, people's number one fear is public speaking. Number two is death. Death is number two. Does that sound right? This means to the average person, if you go to a funeral, you're better off in the casket than doing the eulogy.

It doesn't have to be this way! As a stand-up comedian, one of the most baffling comments I get, aside from "Are you funny?" (seriously, how am I supposed to answer that?!), is, "You are so brave getting up there!"

I speak on behalf of 98% of the stand-up comedians and performers I know who would not describe themselves as brave, except perhaps when attempting to eat the food provided at seedy comedy venues. Now *that* is brave.

With YouTube videos of viral wedding speeches and acts that could be featured on America's Got Talent, there is a lot of unnecessary pressure placed on wedding speeches to somehow be a spectacle – which is soooo not what it should be.

Between you and me, I had a satisfying moment watching a

best man bomb after he told me that comedy "comes naturally to him" and he's going to "ad-lib most of it because it sounds more natural that way". I didn't wish the awkward moments on him, he brought them on himself. The comedy karma rained down upon him because he once said, "It's a genetic fact that women can't be as funny as men." Here's a fact, I do not like this guy, and he doesn't understand what a genetic fact is. Scientist he ain't.

The point is, the dude thought he could wing it, but the first step in being good at anything is practice and preparation, and public speaking is no exception.

You don't have to be an extrovert or professional big mouth like me to prepare a cracking speech. I'm going to give you some tips to ensure that your Maidchilla speech will instead be remembered for being witty, warm, and genuine – just like you!

BE PREPARED

The success of smashing out a memorable speech (or stand-up comedy routine) is due to two things: preparation and authenticity. I know it is easier said than done, but it is way more effort to try to be something you are not, than to get up there and own it as you. Without preparation, you may come off looking foolish or say something that will haunt you to the end of days, just like the ad-libbing best man who made so many schoolboy errors.

PUSHING THE BOUNDARIES...TO A POINT

As a stand-up comedian it's fun to push the boundaries, to explore the taboo. However, a wedding isn't the place to discuss the groom's history of STDs, exes, and divorce. Perhaps you feel deep down inside that the couple isn't '4eva', however the wedding isn't the place to air these feelings, particularly after a couple of glasses of champagne courage. If you really feel strongly about sharing that opinion, do it before the wedding – loooong before the wedding.

Even saying things jokingly, like, "We didn't think you'd last," "We never really liked the bride (or groom)," or "Although we really thought your last boyfriend was tops, we've warmed to the groom," are probably best kept under your hat. Sarcasm is fun, but often deep down these comments may have a kernel of truth and may end up being rather hurtful. So unless they're truly fun and lighthearted, keep the criticisms cool and don't go too hard. It's a speech to wish the couple well, not a roast.

KICK THE NERVES

Nerves are a killer and people often resort to booze to dull them. I can say in all my years of standing up and telling jokes to strangers, I have never drank and talked. Don't get me wrong, I love a tipple, but when I am on stage, I am at work. You don't drink at your desk – or do you?! I prefer to be fully in charge of my brain and mouth, knowing that I can cope with hecklers, dud microphones, and whatever other challenges are thrown in my path.

I'm not saying you have to be Sober Sally on the day, just don't get hammered before you get up there. You might think you're fun and hilarious while tanked but that is not always the case. Breathing, although obvious for the continuation of life, is also an excellent nerve-buster and freak-out-diminisher.

Gentle breaths are best, just make sure they are not directly into the microphone or you'll sound like you're from a 1-800 number. Sometimes before I go on stage I like to say a little mantra to myself, "You can do this!" or, "Even though you didn't get into acting school, you're still an excellent performer!" Try not to let anyone else overhear you saying this though, and make sure the microphone is OFF. I cannot stress this last point enough. OFF!

WHAT DO YOU WANT TO ACHIEVE?

When you are writing the speech (months in advance because you have taken note of my first point: be prepared!), a delicate mix of sincerity and humor is ideal. You may end up with some mild face-palm moments, but try to avoid incurring any cocktail fork stabbings afterwards. I'm supposed to say go for heart over laughs, but really, laughs are what I want. Sweet, sweet laughs. The perfect speech is 90% laughs, 10% heart.

I once endured 25 minutes of the groom using his speech as a sort of verbal LinkedIn presentation, talking about how lucky the bride was to have him. It was gross. Think about your audience. It's family and friends. You are there to celebrate love and the coming together of two wonderful humans. Save the sex stories for the bachelor and bachelorette parties. Grandma has only got a few years left, and she doesn't need a detailed account of her grandson dry humping a pregnant stripper while wearing a moose costume, no matter how funny/tragic that is.

A SIMPLE SPEECH STRUCTURE

- Introduction
- How you met, possibly with an anecdote
- A memory
- Something funny
- How they met their partner
- Why they work well together
- Why you love your friend
- Wish them the best – cheers!

NOTES

A good friend will help you move. But a best friend will help you move a dead body.

Jim Hayes

Be a Great Friend...
That Is All...

MY PARTING ADVICE TO YOU, my Maidchilla friend, is that beyond all expectations of party planning and corralling other Maidchillas, the only really important thing for you to do is to show up and be a friend.

LISTEN TO YOUR BRIDECHILLA FRIEND

Understand her concerns, if she has any, be kind, and try to let any potential nonsense and silly stuff wash over you.

Yes, sometimes you might want to pack a bag and drive across the border, but ultimately the whole experience should come back to you being there to celebrate with your Bridechilla friend.

BE HAPPY FOR YOUR FRIEND

More than which dress to wear and whose Costco card you are using to buy the discount booze for the bachelorette party, being a Maidchilla is about celebrating your friendship and love for your Bridechilla friend.

It's about saying, "We've been through a lot together and we'll go through a bunch more."

You've seen many hairstyles and boyfriends and girlfriends come and go. As friends, you put up with each other's shit, you comfort and protect, you help decipher the true, deep meaning behind DMs. You share private jokes and can be honest about how you feel, your goals, your fears and when things don't go to plan, you have someone to call in the middle of the night that you know will pick up and be there for you.

Your Bridechilla friend may be stressed, she may feel occasionally overwhelmed by the process, opinions and family, but the greatest gift you can give beyond 'bride tribe' sashes and vodka shots is to be there for her. Be mindful, be positive, and be your fucking best self!

Good luck, Maidchilla!

NOTES

We'll be best friends forever because you already know too much.

Anonymous

The Bridechilla Field & Survival Guides

Use codeword **MAIDCHILLA** and get **15%** off!

If you found this guide helpful, then hold on to your hats – there's more!

The Bridechilla Field Guide contains all the lists, questions, and logistical details you need to plan your wedding without losing your chill. It's the fill-out-able must-have for modern couples who want to organize like a boss.

The Bridechilla Survival Guide covers all stages of wedding planning, from dealing with wedding donors (parents who give you money), to ditching obligation guests and meaningless details (so long garters and fuck chair covers). It will free you from wedstress and the quest for perfection.

Written by Bridechilla founder and podcast host Aleisha McCormack, these two guides aren't your regular wedding planner books. You will find wedding planning chill, value, and guidance in these pages.

Visit **www.thebridechilla.com** to get your copy.

ALEISHA MCCORMACK

Aleisha is an Australian comedian, podcaster, and TV producer. She has worked as a writer and presenter for popular Australian comedy, panel, and lifestyle programs, including Channel 10's *The Circle* and *The Project*.

Performing solo stand up comedy shows at international comedy festivals, Aleisha also toured the country with her one-woman show *How To Get Rich*, based on the adventures of meeting her husband Rich (they met on the internet and Aleisha flew across the world on a whim, from Melbourne to London, to meet him for the first time).

Rich and Aleisha got hitched in Melbourne in an intimate DIY wedding in 2012. Surprised by the level of A1 bullshit surrounding the wedding industry and additional pressure placed on couples to plan a "perfect day", Aleisha was inspired to start The Bridechilla Podcast, to empower like-minded couples to plan their own wedding without losing their sanity.

Having produced hundreds of podcast episodes and built a community of free-thinking Bridechillas from all over the world, Aleisha is delighted and surprised that what she started has become a movement.

She resides in London with her current trophy husband Rich, and her drink of choice is vodka, lime, and soda. She's a reformed Nutella addict and her drunk party trick is doing the splits.

FUCK
PERFECT

Bridechilla Founder Aleisha McCormack

NOTES

NOTES

NOTES

NOTES